OUTREACH
SHARING THE WHOLE GOSPEL WITH THE WORLD

FOUNDATIONS FOR
CHRISTIAN LIVING
SERIES

BRINGING TRUTH TO LIFE
NavPress Publishing Group
P.O. Box 35001, Colorado Springs, Colorado 80935

The Navigators is an international Christian organization. Our mission is to reach, disciple, and equip people to know Christ and to make Him known through successive generations. We envision multitudes of diverse people in the United States and every other nation who have a passionate love for Christ, live a lifestyle of sharing Christ's love, and multiply spiritual laborers among those without Christ.

NavPress is the publishing ministry of The Navigators. NavPress publications help believers learn biblical truth and apply what they learn to their lives and ministries. Our mission is to stimulate spiritual formation among our readers.

© 1997 by The Navigators
All rights reserved. No part of this publication may be reproduced in any
    form without written permission from NavPress, P.O. Box 35001,
    Colorado Springs, CO 80935.
ISBN 1-57683-012-8

Cover Photo: Cover Image, © 1997 Photo Disc, Inc.

The FOUNDATIONS FOR CHRISTIAN LIVING (FCL) series grew out of The Navigators' worldwide Scriptural Roots of the Ministry (SRM) process. The eight guides in this series reflect the major themes that emerged from ten years of Scriptural study, international dialogue, and prayer. It is the desire of the SRM team that those who follow Jesus Christ be grounded in these fundamental elements of the faith. For more information regarding the SRM process, please write to NavPress at the above address. The FCL series was researched and developed by Don Bartel, John Purvis, and Chuck Steen. The series text was written by Joanne Heim.

Unless otherwise identified, all Scripture quotations in this publication are taken from the *HOLY BIBLE: NEW INTERNATIONAL VERSION* ® (NIV®), Copyright © 1973, 1978, 1984 by International Bible Society, used by permission of Zondervan Publishing House, all rights reserved. The other version used is *The Message* (MSG) by Eugene H. Peterson, © 1993, 1994, 1995, 1996, used by permission of NavPress Publishing Group, all rights reserved.

Printed in the United States of America

1 2 3 4 5 6 7 8 9 10 11 12 13 14 15 / 02 01 00 99 98 97

FOR A FREE CATALOG OF
NAVPRESS BOOKS & BIBLE STUDIES,
CALL 1-800-366-7788 (USA).
IN CANADA, CALL 1-416-499-4615.

CONTENTS

HOW TO USE THIS GUIDE

For those God foreknew he also predestined to be
conformed to the likeness of his Son. . . .

—*Romans 8:29*

A group that is completely focused on its members and never reaches out to others will eventually become stagnant. Like a pond with no outflow, it will cease to give life to its inhabitants. "As the Father has sent me, I am sending you," Jesus told His followers (John 20:21).

But what is involved in being sent? What does God want us to do? Questions like these require that we ask some deeper ones: What is God's agenda in the world? What was Jesus' mission and message? This study will take you into the very heart of God as you discover God's unique call to you as an individual and as a group.

The FOUNDATIONS Process

The FOUNDATIONS series will help you not merely learn about God but also grow in your love for Him. Through the FOUNDATIONS process you'll grow in discovering God, experiencing one another, and serving in the world. Your group will . . .

▶ pursue the mystery of God together and discover ways to draw closer to Him
▶ grow as you learn to be honest and vulnerable with one another, deeply accepting one another
▶ become courageous in helping one another at the point of personal need
▶ discover how to live genuinely in this fast-paced, complex world
▶ design ways to serve God together, as a group

The nine sessions in this study follow a three-stage process:

1. Session 1 introduces you to the FOUNDATIONS series. You'll explore three essential elements of the spiritual life on which the series focuses. You'll also begin to develop relationships with the other people in your small group. Session 1 is the same in all FOUNDATIONS studies. If you have recently used another FOUNDATIONS study with your current group, you may simply review session 1 of this study.
2. Sessions 2 through 7 lead you through a variety of issues related to understanding what the gospel is and isn't, and learning how to communicate it.
3. Sessions 8 and 9 enable you to take stock of what you've studied and consider what you want to do about it. In session 8 you'll discern how the material applies to you as an individual. Your group will offer feedback and support in following through. In session 9 you'll discuss how the material applies to you as a group. Most of the Bible was written to groups of people rather than to individuals, so session 9 may bring your study alive in ways you did not expect. Session 9 will also help you assess your group's progress in becoming a community as you look at unity, intimacy, interdependence, and mission.

A Modular Approach
Each session is divided into four modules or sections.

OVERVIEW

The overview section briefly describes where the session is headed and what your goals will be. The key issue is stated in the paragraph labeled "So, what's the big deal?" This issue will normally be a point of tension between what the Bible teaches and what we commonly experience. The session will then help your group wrestle through that tension together.

Stating the key issue up front risks preempting the Holy Spirit from guiding your group in the direction He wants to take it, but if you remain open to His leading throughout your individual preparation and group meeting, we believe He'll use the material to minister to you in ways you wouldn't have imagined.

ON YOUR OWN (30-60 minutes)

This section includes the passages you should be sure to examine before your group meets. You'll find some questions easy; others will stretch you mentally. We've found that a spiritual person is defined more by the internal questions he or she is asking than by the conclusions he or she has already reached. Mind-stretching questions are ideal for group discussion—be prepared for a lively debate! (And don't overlook the *For Further Study* questions, where we've hidden some of the best material in each session!)

As you work through this material, it will be helpful to remember a few "principles of understanding" that relate to learning about God:

▶ Understanding comes through mental exertion (Proverbs 2:3-5). Make sure you schedule enough preparation time to delve into the topic.

▶ Understanding comes through the soul and spirit (John 4:24). Seek God in your spirit as you study, as well as when you discuss.

▶ Understanding comes through the insight of others (Romans 1:12; Acts 17:11). Ask God to make you discerning so you will hear what He is saying to you through each other.

GROUP DISCOVERY (40-90 minutes)

This will be the discussion portion of your group meeting. It will usually include three sub-sections:
Let's Warm Up: Each group session opens with a question or two to help you learn about each other. The warm-up questions also help you move from what you were thinking about (or worried about) when you arrived at the meeting to what the biblical texts deal with. These questions put you in touch with the topic in an experiential way, so your discussion is not just sharing ideas but sharing life. The questions

in this section always focus on life experiences and are usually fun to answer.

Let's Talk: In this section you'll examine one or two key Bible passages on the topic and discuss what light these passages shed on the central tension of the study. You'll also discuss any questions raised by your individual study. Feel free to bring to the group anything that perplexed or excited you in your individual study.

Let's Act: The questions in this section connect what you've studied to how you live. They often ask you to consider applying what you've learned to your group as a whole, rather than just to your individual life. Application is the reason for Bible study; be sure you allow plenty of time for it.

GROUP WORSHIP   (15-30 minutes)

In order to stress the importance of the worship portion of your meeting, we have set it apart as a special section. Worship and prayer as a group are essential components of the FOUNDATIONS process. Praying and worshiping together can be one of the most faith-building and relationship-building activities you do together. Since many people have never prayed aloud with others before, the suggestions for worship begin gently. Later in the study you'll have an opportunity to plan your own worship times. You may decide to assign one person in the group to plan and lead worship, or you may rotate the responsibility.

In session 4 you'll begin to set aside at least 15 minutes of your worship time to discuss prayerfully and humbly a question often overlooked in Bible studies: "What is the Holy Spirit saying to us?" (This is referred to as **Let's Listen to God**.) You may find it challenging to get past what you imagine God ought to be saying to the group. The experience of trying to discern God's voice will invariably draw your group to a deeper level of intimacy.

Facilitator's Job Description
Leadership is essential to an effective group. FOUNDATIONS studies will go much better if someone in your group takes responsibility to:

1. Launch the group
   ▶ Recruit people for the group, explaining its purpose and process.
   ▶ Schedule meetings (with group consensus).

2. Pray regularly
   ▶ For the individual members in their daily lives.
   ▶ For the group's growth into community.
   ▶ For the courage and faith of the group to take the steps it needs to grow in Christ.

3. Build community
   ▶ Stay in touch with the members, encouraging them to also stay in touch with each other.
   ▶ Make sure that each member grows in his or her ownership of this group. (This can be done by assigning responsibility—those with responsibility usually experience ownership and genuine membership in a group.)
   ▶ Help the group move beyond studying to doing.
   ▶ Maintain momentum and remotivate group members if enthusiasm diminishes.

4. Facilitate rather than lead
   ▶ Search for vision and direction together, rather than announcing vision and answers. Help the group arrive at its vision and answers. Help people go where the Spirit is leading them, rather than where you think they should go. Remind them that understanding is only the beginning; implementing is the goal.
   ▶ Teach by asking questions, rather than making authoritative statements. Questions can often accomplish what statements cannot. Questions were Jesus' preferred style.
   ▶ Draw out the quiet or introverted persons.
   ▶ Encourage everyone's participation; affirm the different contributions of all.

5. Be content with less than ideal progress
   ▶ Put up with some ambiguity. People never grow in a constant or straight line. Two steps forward and one step back is the norm.

Remember what Christ has tolerated in you. Be happy with progress in the general direction of FOUNDATIONS goals.

6. Watch the clock
   ► When the allotted time for a given section is over, go on to the next section even if the group has not exhausted its discussion. (It is likely you will need to do this—many of the **Let's Talk** sections have more than enough material to fill the recommended time slot.) Unless you have unlimited time, the group will appreciate being kept on schedule. Don't allow discussion to consume all of your time so that application and worship must be omitted. On the other hand, if you sense the Spirit of God is actively at work, follow the Spirit's leading, not the clock. Look for an appropriate time at which to say, "I sense that God is doing something important here. Is it okay with all of you if we extend our time in this section of the meeting?"

7. Delegate
   ► After the first two or three sessions, ask someone else in the group to lead the worship time. Someone in your group is probably gifted in the area of worship and interested in helping the group focus on God through worship. Also, ask someone to lead the Group Discovery discussion. Direct that person to read item 4 in this job description. You could rotate this job around the group. Finally, appoint someone else to be timekeeper. By delegating these three functions, you will encourage all participants to feel like owners of the group rather than spectators.

8. Establish ground rules
   ► It is important that everyone in the group has a chance to buy into the rules by which the group will run. Ground rules clarify what the group expects from each person. The most important ground rules are stated on pages 17-18. Be sure to discuss them in your first meeting.

1.
THREE BIG IDEAS

OVERVIEW

In this introductory session you'll examine the three essential elements of the spiritual life on which the FOUNDATIONS series focuses: worship, community, and service. Your goals will be:

► To understand and own these three elements—worship, community, and service
► To get to know each other by telling a little of your stories and why you've joined this group

Session 1 is the same in all FOUNDATIONS studies. If you have recently used another FOUNDATIONS study with your current group, you may choose to do session 1 or merely to review it and then skip to session 2.

ON YOUR OWN   (30-60 minutes)

Most of us would like to love and be loved better than we already do and are. The FOUNDATIONS series revolves around three fundamental commands Jesus gave to His followers:

► Love God with all your heart, soul, mind, and strength (see Mark 12:30).
► Love one another as Jesus loves you (see John 13:34).
► Love your neighbor as yourself (see Mark 12:31).

In these verses, Jesus states the "big picture" of what the spiritual life is about. We love Him through worship, we love one another through community, and we love others through service. We can depict this threefold lifestyle with the following set of concentric circles:

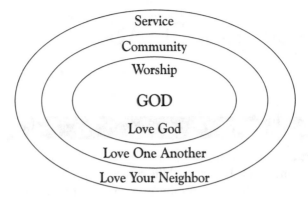

These three commands may be summarized in a single goal for the series:

To help you become a community—a small, closely knit group motivated and empowered to worship and serve God together.

Worship, community, and service form the structural backbone of the FOUNDATIONS process. They will direct your love toward God, toward the others in your group, and toward your neighbors (others not yet a part of your group). At the end of this study, you'll have a chance to summarize what you've learned about worship, community, and service, and to assess your progress as a group toward these three outcomes.

WORSHIP
God's commands about love show that He is vitally interested in relationships and that our relationship with Him should be our highest priority. Worship is the all-consuming, ongoing activity of heaven. We have the inexpressible privilege of joining in the cosmic worship of the King already taking place in the heavenly realm.

When we see God as He is and worship Him, the other areas of our lives begin to work themselves out. Drawing near to God's heart in spirit and truth will inevitably affect our relationships with others.

Hence, worship will become the centerpiece of your group experience. This concentration on God will set your little community apart from a mere discussion group or gathering of friends. While early sessions of this study will include suggestions for worship, feel free to use your entire group's creativity and experience under the leadership of the Holy Spirit as you come into God's presence session by session.

The essence of worship is turning our attention toward God, reflecting His glorious attributes back to Him, and agreeing with who He is and what He has done. God delights to reveal Himself more fully to us as we worship, to satisfy our hearts' desire for relationship with Him, and to give us help for our desperate needs.

God invites us to come to Him with our burdens, needs, joys, and heartaches. In reality, we cannot come to God without our burdens; they are part of who we are. Instead of denying the things on our hearts, we'll find it far more helpful to acknowledge them as fully as possible, commit them to God, then seek Him in His greatness for who He is.

1. When you think of worship, what ideas or images come to mind?
   ☐ lively music
   ☐ majestic hymns or choral works
   ☐ silence and solitude
   ☐ lengthy sermons
   ☐ performers and spectators
   ☐ communing with nature in the woods or by a stream
   ☐ all of life
   ☐ other:

2. On a scale of 1 to 10, how would you rate your most recent experience of worship in terms of how well it focused your heart on God's greatness? Why?

1	2	3	4	5	6	7	8	9	10
dry				okay					awesome

3. Does the idea of worship being the centerpiece of your group experience attract or trouble you? Why?

COMMUNITY

From a centered place of loving God, you'll move outward to loving the others in your group. This shared life is what the New Testament writers mean by *koinonia*: "fellowship," "communion," "partnership," "participation," "community."

> We saw it, we heard it, and now we're telling you so you can experience it along with us, this experience of communion with the Father and his Son, Jesus Christ. Our motive for writing is simply this: We want you to enjoy this, too. Your joy will double our joy! (1 John 1:3-4, MSG)

In the FOUNDATIONS series we assume that dynamic Christian community as described in the New Testament is not only possible but normative for us. When we fail to experience such relationships, we miss the fullness of life that God intends for us. While there are many spiritually important things one can and should do alone, an effective community contributes equally crucial ingredients of life. People in community can:

> ► encourage one another in good times and bad
> ► ask thoughtful questions when a member has a decision to make
> ► listen to God together
> ► learn how to pray together and for one another
> ► benefit from one another's insights into Scripture
> ► acquire a habit of reading the Bible
> ► practice loving their neighbors
> ► worship God together
> ► learn to communicate effectively and solve problems together
> ► learn to receive care from others
> ► experience the pleasure of helping another person grow

Community in these studies refers to a small group of 3 to 13 people who relate in a certain way. Community in this sense is very different from any organizational form or structure. Matthew 18:20 says, "For where there are two or three who have been joined together into my Name with the result that I am the common object of their faith, there I am in their midst."[1] The individuals together are seeking intimacy with God and fellowship with each other. *Koinonia* includes partnership, participation, and contribution. It implies communication and vulnerability. It is much more than just getting together and discussing some nonvolatile topic.

Jesus wanted His disciples to experience a unique relationship when they came together—unique in their love for and their unity with one another. When genuine love is present, a group has taken the first and biggest step toward real community. This process is not easy. Your group will probably have to resolve a number of relational issues on the road to biblical community.

4. What appeals to you about this description of community?

5. What questions or concerns do you have about this kind of community? Explain.

SERVICE

Any community focused on God loves to serve both believers and unbelievers, just as God does. How could it be otherwise? You'll find that as your group grows in worshiping God and loving one another, the members will intuitively know they need to be helping others. This will be natural.

What may not be natural is serving together as a team and serving the lost—both of which Jesus did and which His followers throughout history have done.

Most of us slowly abandon former friends and acquaintances when we join the kingdom of God. We're not comfortable anymore around those who do not share our new values. Our old friends no longer feel comfortable around us. Somehow we lose the ability Jesus had to be "a friend of tax collectors and 'sinners'" (Matthew 11:19). It is far easier for us to serve those within the kingdom of God than those more distant.

And if somehow we do seek to draw the lost toward Christ, we usually do so as individuals, rather than in partnership with other believers. Consequently, those who need the Savior never experience the powerful influence of a loving community.

The FOUNDATIONS studies will guide your group into these two dimensions: serving the lost and serving together. Serving does not exclusively mean explaining the gospel verbally. Loving our neighbor often translates into specific acts of compassionate service at home, neighborhood, or work. We often serve individually, but this FOUNDATIONS guide will focus your efforts on serving God's interests together. You will not be told what to do; you will not be pushed beyond your point of willing consent. Rather, you will decide together how to put what you are studying into practice outside your group.

6. What thoughts and feelings does this description of service raise for you?
   ☐ Excitement—I'm ready to go!
   ☐ Discomfort—The last thing I need is more on my "to-do" list.
   ☐ Anxiety—I did door-to-door witnessing several years ago and hated it. Will we have to do that again?
   ☐ Ambivalence—I have a strong desire to serve more, but I know it's not easy for me.
   ☐ Confusion—Isn't it good enough for us just to take care of each other for awhile?
   ☐ Relief—I'm glad this isn't just another navel-gazing group.
   ☐ Other (explain):

7. Is this statement true of you: "It is far easier for us to serve those within the kingdom of God than those more distant." If so, why do you think that is?

8. We have stated three priorities: loving God, loving others in the group, and loving others outside the group. What about loving yourself? Do you think this should be a priority ahead of any or all of these three? Explain your view.

 GROUP DISCOVERY (40-90 minutes)

Let's Warm Up (10 minutes)
Beginning with the leader, let each person take one minute to answer question 9.

9. Recall an important friendship from your childhood. Who was that friend, and what was special about that friendship? What bond kept you and that friend together?

Let's Talk (30 minutes)
10. Share your responses to questions 1-8 in the "On Your Own" section. Discuss any questions you have about the three big ideas stated there.

11. Discuss the following ground rules for your group. Feel free to change anything. The objective is for everyone to be content with the result, not for everyone to go along while harboring private reservations.
   ☐ Purpose: The reason our group exists is to become a community—a small, closely knit group motivated and empowered to worship and serve God.
   ☐ Participation: I am committed to participating in this community, to worshiping, and to serving others outside the group.
   ☐ Attendance: I will be here as often as possible. This group will be a priority.
   ☐ Ownership: I agree to share responsibility for our group goals.

☐ Confidentiality: I agree to keep here whatever is shared here.
☐ Accountability: I agree to give permission to the other group members to hold me accountable for goals I set for myself.
☐ Accessibility: I give group members permission to call me when they are in need—even in the middle of the night. My phone number is. . . .

GROUP WORSHIP (15-30 minutes)

12. Pray that God would begin to reveal Himself in more of His majesty, power, and direction.

13. Read Psalm 89:1-18 aloud together. When you are through, allow a moment of silence for everyone to focus on God. In worship, you have no agenda but to focus on Him.

14. Beginning with the leader, let each person thank God for one thing he or she learned in this session, or praise God for one aspect of Himself highlighted in your discussion. If you are comfortable doing so, allow for additional, spontaneous expressions of thanks and praise.

Optional
If you think your group might appreciate singing together, ask someone to lead with guitar or other instrument. If no one in your group has that skill, consider singing with a CD; some are now designed especially for small group worship. Be sure the person who leads worship understands that singing is only one aspect of worship, and that he or she should limit singing to the time allotted in your schedule.

---

1. Wuest, Kenneth S. *The New Testament: An Expanded Translation.* Grand Rapids, Mich.: Eerdmans, 1961.

2.
GOD'S INTEREST IN THE WORLD

For God so loved the world that he gave his one and only
Son, that whoever believes in him shall not perish but
have eternal life.

—*John 3:16*

OVERVIEW

Many people believe that God is like a clockmaker—
He created the world, wound it up, and sat back to watch it from a
distance. But the Bible tells a different story of God's involvement in
the world. It teaches that God is immensely interested in the world
and has been involved with its people since time began.

In this lesson, you will learn how God established nations and cultures. By examining a variety of Bible passages, you'll learn what it
means to be an alien or outsider and how you should relate to others
around you. You'll also see how much God values the variety of cultures around the world. Your goal is to assess how well you relate to
people of other cultures.

So, what's the big deal?

God created diversity—nations, races, and cultures. As followers of
Christ, we lean toward conformity and sometimes assume that all
believers should be basically the same. How do we break free from our
tendency and reach out to people who are different?

Genesis tells the story of how and why people spread across the earth and divided into cultural groupings. Culture is an integrated system of a people whose language, habits, and customs give them identity and distinction from others. A nation is similar and is typically defined as a large community of people of mainly common descent, language, and history who usually inhabit a particular territory and are under one government. However, today many nations—such as Canada, the United States, Great Britain, Russia, India, and Turkey—include citizens from several cultures with different languages and histories.

1. Describe some characteristics of your culture.

After the Flood (Genesis 6–9), the eight members of Noah's family were given a command: "As for you, be fruitful and increase in number; multiply on the earth and increase upon it" (Genesis 9:7). Genesis 10 traces the genealogy of Noah's family and how they were divided into different nations.

It's easy to see this passage as simply a list of unfamiliar names and places. However, by using ancient documents and inscriptions that mention these nations' names, their locations have all been identified with reasonable accuracy. In general, the descendants of Shem are Semitic (including Jews and Arabs), the Japhethites are Indo-Europeans, and the Hamites are Africans and the now-extinct Canaanites.

2. Read Genesis 10:1-32. From this passage, how were the nations created?

Genesis 11:1-9 took place before the nations had spread too far. Some scholars estimate the story of Babel occurred around 4000 B.C., or perhaps earlier. At the time, people typically lived in stone-walled cities, each with its own cult. Eventually, these communities began to unite under one cult with one priest-king and one temple. The tower of Babel was built in this kind of kingdom.

The ruins of a tower still stand on the site (tradition suggests this was not the original tower, but a later one). The base was built of mud bricks and tar in seven stages, like a staircase-hill. Each stage was painted a color to correspond with one of the gods—black for Saturn, orange for Jupiter, and so on. The top of the tower was painted with the signs of the zodiac, in which the priests sought to reach the heavens by magical rites. The ruins that remain once stood 153 feet high and covered nearly four acres.

> Now the whole world had one language and a common speech. As men moved eastward, they found a plain in Shinar and settled there.
>
> They said to each other, "Come, let's make bricks and bake them thoroughly." They used brick instead of stone, and tar for mortar. Then they said, "Come, let us build ourselves a city, with a tower that reaches to the heavens, so that we may make a name for ourselves and not be scattered over the face of the whole earth."
>
> But the LORD came down to see the city and the tower that the men were building. The LORD said, "If as one people speaking the same language they have begun to do this, then nothing they plan to do will be impossible for them. Come, let us go down and confuse their language so they will not understand each other."
>
> So the LORD scattered them from there over all the

earth, and they stopped building the city. That is why it was called Babel—because there the LORD confused the language of the whole world. From there the LORD scattered them over the face of the whole earth. (Genesis 11:1-9)

3. Why did the people build this tower?

4. How would you describe their motivation to build the tower?
   ☐ Selfish
   ☐ Utilitarian
   ☐ Logical
   ☐ Foolish
   ☐ Smart
   ☐ Arrogant
   ☐ Other (please explain):

5. How did God respond to their building the tower?

6. Why do you think God responded the way He did?

In the book of Acts, we read about Paul's visit to the Greek city of Athens. As he walks around the city, he grows increasingly distressed at the number of idols in the city, but is also intrigued by one dedicated to "an unknown God." He is then overjoyed to introduce the Athenians to God—who wants to be known by all.

From one man he made every nation of men, that they
should inhabit the whole earth; and he determined the
times set for them and the exact places where they should
live. God did this so that men would seek him and perhaps
reach out for him and find him, though he is not far from
each one of us. (Acts 17:26-27)

7. What reason does Paul give for the variety of nations?

8. How does God's reason for creating nations help explain the story
   of Babel?

After God created different nations and languages, He promised
Abraham that he would be the father of His chosen nation. Despite
this promise, God didn't simply forget about all those other nations. In
fact, His purpose in setting apart a chosen nation was to bless others
through that nation.

> "I will make you into a great nation
>   and I will bless you;
> I will make your name great,
>   and you will be a blessing.
> I will bless those who bless you,
>   and whoever curses you I will curse;
> and all peoples on earth
>   will be blessed through you." (Genesis 12:2-3)

9. How has God blessed all nations through Abraham's descendants?

10. From your study of Genesis and Acts, how would you describe God's attitude toward nations and cultures around the world?

11. Do you think God wants people around the world to give up their culture for one more closely resembling the Judeo-Christian culture of many Western nations? Explain your answer.

12. As a believer, you are a member of God's chosen people. All believers everywhere are "a chosen people, a royal priesthood, a holy nation, a people belonging to God, that you may declare the praises of him who called you out of darkness into his wonderful light" (1 Peter 2:9). What's our job according to Peter?

13. How concerned are you about being a blessing to "all the peoples on earth"?
    - ☐ It's not something I've thought about before.
    - ☐ I want to be a blessing to nonbelievers and share the gospel with them, but I'm not sure how.
    - ☐ I'm always looking for opportunities to reach out to nonbelievers.
    - ☐ I like the idea, but does that mean I have to be a missionary?
    - ☐ Other (please explain):

For Further Study
Trace God's interest in the nations and His commitment to them throughout the Bible.

- ▶ Genesis 22:15-18
- ▶ Joshua 4:23-24
- ▶ Isaiah 49:1-7 (also see Acts 13:46-48)
- ▶ Jonah 3:1—4:11
- ▶ Galatians 3:26-29
- ▶ Revelation 7:9-10

 GROUP DISCOVERY (50-90 minutes)

Let's Warm Up (10 minutes)

14. Have you ever been to a place where you didn't speak the language? How did you feel?

Let's Talk (30-50 minutes)

15. Discuss your answers to the "On Your Own" questions. What did you learn about culture? About nations? About yourself?

16. The term "alien" appears throughout the Bible. Aliens are out-siders—strangers, pilgrims, sojourners, and visitors. Take a few minutes and think of the outsiders you see. How would you describe them?

- ☐ Homeless
- ☐ Poor
- ☐ Foreign
- ☐ Lonely
- ☐ New to town
- ☐ Difficult
- ☐ Rich
- ☐ Immigrants
- ☐ Racially different
- ☐ Hungry
- ☐ Other (please explain):

17. How do you usually treat these people when you're around them?

The Israelites were resident aliens (non-citizens) in Egypt for 400 years and were oppressed because of ethnic differences. Then God liberated them and gave them land in Palestine. But Palestine remained a land of various cultures and backgrounds. Many of the Bible passages about aliens provide solutions to the tensions that cropped up between aliens and the people they relied on. In most of the Old Testament passages, God's people were not the aliens, but those who accepted strangers into their midst. The laws refer to Israel's historical experience as an oppressed people.

18. Read the following passages out loud, underlining key words that describe how God told Israel to treat outsiders.

> "Do not oppress an alien; you yourselves know how it feels to be aliens, because you were aliens in Egypt." (Exodus 23:9)

> "When an alien lives with you in your land, do not mistreat him. The alien living with you must be treated as one of your native-born. Love him as yourself, for you were aliens in Egypt. I am the LORD your God." (Leviticus 19:33-34)

> "The community is to have the same rules for you and for the alien living among you; this is a lasting ordinance for the generations to come. You and the alien shall be the same before the LORD." (Numbers 15:15)

> He defends the cause of the fatherless and the widow, and loves the alien, giving him food and clothing. And you are to love those who are aliens, for you yourselves were aliens in Egypt. (Deuteronomy 10:18-19)

Cursed is the man who withholds justice from the alien, the fatherless or the widow. (Deuteronomy 27:19)

Do not oppress the widow or the fatherless, the alien or the poor. In your hearts do not think evil of each other. (Zechariah 7:10)

"So I will come near to you for judgment. I will be quick to testify against sorcerers, adulterers and perjurers, against those who defraud laborers of their wages, who oppress the widows and the fatherless, and deprive aliens of justice, but do not fear me," says the LORD Almighty. (Malachi 3:5)

19. What is God's attitude toward aliens or outsiders?

20. Why were these laws necessary?

21. How do you think God would have us treat the following people?

☐ Foreign students

☐ Illegal aliens

☐ Legal immigrants

☐ Those people born in your country, but of a different culture

22. How easy is it for you to treat outsiders the way God treats them?
    (1 = easy; 10 = difficult)

1	2	3	4	5	6	7	8	9	10
easy									difficult

Eventually the Jews were scattered through the Mediterranean area and the Middle East and became aliens in those countries. And when people followed Christ, they also became aliens. The Bible says that followers of Christ are aliens and strangers in this world because their true home is with God.

> Dear friends, I urge you, as aliens and strangers in the world, to abstain from sinful desires, which war against your soul. Live such good lives among the pagans that, though they accuse you of doing wrong, they may see your good deeds and glorify God on the day he visits us.
> (1 Peter 2:11-12)

> But our citizenship is in heaven. And we eagerly await a Savior from there, the Lord Jesus Christ. (Philippians 3:20)

23. Do you relate to any of the characteristics or examples of being an alien or outsider that you've already discussed? Explain.

Living as an alien is vital to faith. The writer of Hebrews included a hall of fame for people of great faith in his letter. These heroes of the faith provide us with examples of living right before God. One thing they all had in common was the understanding that they were outsiders in this world.

> All these people were still living by faith when they died. They did not receive the things promised; they only saw

them and welcomed them from a distance. And they
admitted that they were aliens and strangers on earth.
People who say such things show that they are looking for a
country of their own. If they had been thinking of the
country they had left, they would have had opportunity to
return. Instead, they were longing for a better country—a
heavenly one. Therefore God is not ashamed to be called
their God, for he has prepared a city for them.
(Hebrews 11:13-16)

24. How would it affect your life to admit that you are an alien and a
stranger in this world?

25. Does knowing that you're an outsider make it easier for you to
relate to the aliens and outsiders you come into contact with? If
so, how?

Let's Act (15-30 minutes)

26. As a group, mentally walk around your neighborhood and/or office
and note the people from various nations, cultures, world views, socio-
economic backgrounds, et cetera. Discuss the people around you who:
   - ☐ speak the same language, come from the same basic cultural
     heritage, think similarly about values and spiritual realities
   - ☐ speak the same language and come from the same basic cul-
     tural heritage, yet think differently about life, values, and
     spiritual realities
   - ☐ speak a different language and/or come from different cultural
     background, but think similarly about values and spiritual
     realities
   - ☐ both speak a different language and/or come from different
     cultural background, and also think differently about life,
     values and spiritual realities

27. How can you begin to develop relationships with those people?

28. As a result of your discussion, what might the Holy Spirit be communicating to your group about the following things? (Think about the Holy Spirit's message to you as a group, rather than to each of you as individuals.)

☐ Your worship

☐ Your relationships as a group

☐ Your responsibilities/relationships with others (neighbors, coworkers, family, seekers, new believers, disciples, enemies)

 GROUP WORSHIP   **(15-30 minutes)**

29. Read Psalm 47 together as a group.

30. If your group is so inclined, sing an appropriate song or chorus praising God.

31. Spend some time praying that God would help you identify more closely with those who are not like you. Pray that He would give you opportunities to develop relationships with those people you identified earlier in the "Let's Act" section.

3.

GOD'S PURSUIT OF THE LOST

The Lord is not slow in keeping his promise, as some
understand slowness. He is patient with you, not wanting
anyone to perish, but everyone to come to repentance.

—2 Peter 3:9

OVERVIEW

God's interest in the world doesn't end with creating
nations and caring for outsiders. In 2 Peter 3:9 we learn that God
doesn't want anyone to perish, but wants everyone to have a saving
relationship with Him. God uses people to reach the lost. In sessions 3
and 4 we will look at two groups through whom God reaches lost
people—through those called to an apostolic function and those called
to local ministry.

To reach those outside our cultural or national boundaries, God
has sent apostles. In this lesson, you will examine Paul's life and learn
what an apostle really is. Then you'll determine whether your calling to
reach unbelievers is an apostolic or a local one.

So, what's the big deal?

Jesus commanded all believers to share the gospel. But some believers
are called to be apostles and to cross cultural or national boundaries to
reach others for Christ. Others are called to work locally among nonbelievers. How can we know what we've been called to when it comes
to sharing the gospel?

The word "apostle" comes from the Greek word *apostelos* (*apo* means "from" and *stello* means "to send"). Under Jewish law in the first century A.D., an apostle was someone sent on a mission to represent the sender. An apostle could collect religious taxes, deliver a certificate of divorce, or even stand in for the bridegroom in a betrothal.

When the writer to the Hebrews called Jesus "the apostle and high priest whom we confess" (Hebrews 3:1), he was saying that God had sent Jesus as the Father's apostle (proxy, representative) to humans.

Then Jesus appointed twelve men to be His apostles, His official representatives on earth when He returned to the Father. The apostles had the same mission Jesus had: to proclaim the kingdom of God and invite people to join it (Luke 9:1-2, John 20:21-23). After Judas betrayed Jesus, 120 of Jesus' followers chose one among them named Matthias to be the twelfth apostle (Acts 1:12-26). They wanted twelve apostles to match the twelve tribes of Israel, for the Twelve would symbolize the new Israel.

The Twelve were apostles in a unique sense because they had known Jesus well during His time on earth and had all seen Him after His resurrection. The early church recognized their exclusive, special authority.

Later, however, other people were recognized as apostles in a wider sense, including:

- ▶ Barnabas (Acts 14:1-4,14)
- ▶ Andronicus and Junias (Romans 16:7; Junias is a woman's name in all other ancient references, so this was probably a woman)
- ▶ Apollos (1 Corinthians 3:21-22; 4:6,9)
- ▶ Timothy and Silas (1 Thessalonians 1:1, 2:6-7)
- ▶ probably James (Galatians 1:19)
- ▶ Paul (Acts 14:1-4,14; 1 Corinthians 9:1-3)

Paul repeatedly clashed with other people who claimed to be apostles, but who Paul said were false apostles (2 Corinthians 11:5,13; 12:11). Thus, the term "apostle" had several shades of meaning that implied varying degrees of authority.

Paul is the apostle we know most about. His authority came to be regarded as equal to that of the Twelve in that Jesus appeared to him personally (1 Corinthians 15:1-8) and gave him primary responsibility to bring the gospel to the Gentiles (Ephesians 3:2-7). Although he called himself "the least of the apostles" (1 Corinthians 15:9), he knew he had been given special authority, and the church eventually recognized his writings as part of the Word of God.

When most people today think of apostles, they think of the Twelve and Paul, a unique group. If we think the functions of apostles were to write Scripture and in other ways lay the foundations of the church, then we will see no need of apostles today. However, some apostolic functions are still relevant today. In this session you will investigate some of these functions and consider how they might be relevant today.

1. Who else comes to mind when you think of an apostle?

Hebrews 3:1 calls Jesus the "apostle and high priest whom we confess." Throughout the Gospels, Jesus repeatedly claimed to have been sent from God. Jesus in turn sent His disciples into the world and gave them specific instructions, called the Great Commission, about what they were to accomplish while He was gone.

> Then the eleven disciples went to Galilee, to the mountain where Jesus had told them to go. When they saw him, they worshiped him; but some doubted. Then Jesus came to them and said, "All authority in heaven and on earth has been given to me. Therefore go and make disciples of all nations, baptizing them in the name of the Father and of the Son and of the Holy Spirit, and teaching them to obey everything I have commanded you. And surely I am with you always, to the very end of the age."
> (Matthew 28:16-20)

2. Circle all of the verbs in Jesus' instructions to the Eleven. What did Jesus command them to do?

3. How is it possible for this to work? (What kinds of people does it take?)

4. Which of the following activities from the Great Commission have you done or participated in?
   ☐ Gone anywhere for the purpose of spreading the gospel
   ☐ Made disciples
   ☐ Baptized people
   ☐ Taught people to obey all of God's commands

5. Look at the boxes you didn't check. Why do you think you haven't done them?

6. To whom do you believe the Great Commission applies?
   ☐ The eleven disciples
   ☐ All believers
   ☐ Those called to be apostles
   ☐ Other (please explain):

7. Do you think you can obey the Great Commission right where you are now, or do you have to leave home? Explain.

Paul is one of the most well-known apostles and is often used as an example of what an apostle should be. In the passage below, Paul is telling King Agrippa the story of how God called him to be an apostle. He began his story by telling King Agrippa about his background. Paul was a staunch Jew all his life and was well-known for his persecution of Christ's followers. Paul was a Pharisee, one of a pious Jewish sect who advocated minute obedience to the Jewish law and traditions. As such, he believed that the Messiah would come to save only the Jews. Paul's Jewish name was Saul; Paul (or Paulus) was his Roman name.

> We all fell to the ground, and I heard a voice saying to me in Aramaic, "Saul, Saul, why do you persecute me? It is hard for you to kick against the goads."
> Then I asked, "Who are you, Lord?"
> "I am Jesus, whom you are persecuting," the Lord replied. "Now get up and stand on your feet. I have appeared to you to appoint you as a servant and as a witness of what you have seen of me and what I will show you. I will rescue you from your own people and from the Gentiles. I am sending you to them to open their eyes and turn them from darkness to light, and from the power of Satan to God, so that they may receive forgiveness of sins and a place among those who are sanctified by faith in me." (Acts 26:14-18)

8. What did Jesus tell Paul he was supposed to do?

9. How does Paul's description of his calling match the definition of an apostle?

Not everyone can reach across cultural barriers and be an apostle. Paul had a unique gift to minister to those outside his culture. Paul explains his secret for reaching people in 1 Corinthians.

> Though I am free and belong to no man, I make myself a slave to everyone, to win as many as possible. To the Jews I became like a Jew, to win the Jews. To those under the law I became like one under the law (though I myself am not under the law), so as to win those under the law. To those not having the law I became like one not having the law (though I am not free from God's law but am under Christ's law), so as to win those not having the law. To the weak I became weak, to win the weak. I have become all things to all men so that by all possible means I might save some. I do all this for the sake of the gospel, that I may share in its blessings. (1 Corinthians 9:19-23)

10. How did Paul reach people for Christ?

11. Why would this be an effective method of evangelism?

Not all people are equally flexible with respect to cultural differences. To help you think about your own flexibility regarding cultural differences, answer the following questions:

12. List the different cultures you see residing in this country.

13. List as many dominant cultures from around the world as you can think of.

14. Assess your attitudes toward people of other cultures by asking yourself the following questions about each of the cultures you listed above. (Simply mark the appropriate letter next to each culture you listed above. Remember, this is an assessment, not a test; it's better to answer honestly than correctly.)
    a. I enjoy being around people from this culture.
    b. I appreciate the good I see in this culture.
    c. I don't understand this culture.
    d. I don't see much good at all in this culture.
    e. I'm strongly biased against anyone from this culture.

For Further Study
Read about others whom the New Testament designates as apostles:

▶ Barnabas (Acts 14:1-4,14),
▶ Andronicus and Junias (Romans 16:7),
▶ Apollos (1 Corinthians 3:21-22; 4:6,9),
▶ James, the Lord's brother (Galatians 1:19), and
▶ Timothy (1 Thessalonians 1:1; 2:6-7)

Look up other passages in which Jesus commissions His followers: Mark 16:15-18, John 20:21-23, Acts 1:8.

GROUP DISCOVERY

Let's Warm Up (10 minutes)

15. If you could be sent on a special assignment anywhere in the world, where would you want to go and what would you want to do?

Let's Talk (30-50 minutes)

16. Discuss your answers to the "On Your Own" questions. Did your understanding of what it means to be an apostle change? How?

17. We tend to think of apostles in terms of missionaries. What are some of the stereotypes your group has about missionaries?
    ☐ They live in the jungle.
    ☐ They're poor.
    ☐ They live without modern conveniences.
    ☐ They're more godly than I am.
    ☐ They received a special calling—one that I haven't received.
    ☐ They are imposing our culture on people of other cultures.
    ☐ They work very hard with little to show for it.
    ☐ There are snakes and bugs everywhere.
    ☐ Other (please explain):

It's easy to think of apostles like Paul and Peter or missionaries living in the jungle without running water. But what does it really look like to fulfill an apostolic role in today's world? Read the following stories, noting the things they have in common.

Kristen was involved with a parachurch organization all through college and loved meeting and sharing with other believers. After graduation, she decided to take advantage of an opportunity to spend a year in France, working among international students along with a team. She is excited to share Christ with others who may have never heard the gospel before and who come from a wide range of cultural, religious, and social backgrounds. She plans to return to the United States after the year is over and work as an accountant.

Michael always wanted to be a missionary. He loved reading about them when he was younger and couldn't wait to grow up and follow in their footsteps. He's now living in a developing country, reaching people who may never have known a follower of Christ before. His team consists of himself, another single man, and a married couple. Michael knows he's doing what God called him to do, but thinks of it more as living his childhood dream.

Scott and his family were living in the suburbs when they started working at a local soup kitchen together. As they began to develop relationships with many of the people who came in for a meal, Scott wished there was a way to increase his level of interaction with the people they met there. After much prayer, Scott and his family decided to move into the city. There they contribute to others' needs as members of the community, not as outsiders who don't understand what life there is like. It's not been easy, but the relationships they've built over the past two years have been well worth it.

18. Kristen, Michael, and Scott are all fulfilling apostolic functions. What common elements do you see in each of their experiences?

19. Do you think they could do their ministries alone? Explain.

Not everyone is called to an apostolic ministry (reaching out to others across cultural boundaries). Some are called to minister locally (reaching out to people within your same culture). It's important to determine whether God has called you to an apostolic ministry or a local ministry.

20. In the "On Your Own" section, you learned about Paul's flexibility in relating to people of other cultures. As you have thought about yourself, do you think you tend to be more or less comfortable moving across cultural boundaries? Place yourself on the scale below.

1	2	3	4	5	6	7	8	9	10
not comfortable at all								very comfortable	

21. How much contact have you had with other cultures?

22. How do you usually react when the rules for behavior are suddenly changed?

23. Another way to determine if your calling is apostolic or local is to look at your own interests. How interested would you be in actually moving into another culture and being part of it in order to reach others?

1	2	3	4	5	6	7	8	9	10
not interested								very interested	

24. a. Has being an apostle in this sense been something you've thought about in the past, but never acted on?

    b. Have other people suggested this kind of ministry for you?

25. Do you think God might be calling you to an apostolic ministry? Why do you say that?

Let's Act (15-30 minutes)

26. a. As a result of this discussion, what might the Holy Spirit be communicating to your group about its calling? (Think about the Holy Spirit's message to you as a group, rather than to each of you as individuals.)

    b. Are there individuals in the group who sense a calling different from the group in general? If so, what can the group do to support someone with that calling?

27. How does your calling as individuals affect your relationships with others (neighbors, coworkers, family, seekers, new believers, disciples, enemies)?

28. Praise God that He cares about all the people on earth and has sent out apostles to reach them. Ask Him for ways you can be part of reaching lost people.

29. Spend time praying for the people you know who are carrying the gospel across cultural or national boundaries. Pray that God would be near to them and that He would comfort them, as they may be far away from friends and family.

30. If your group is so inclined, sing an appropriate song or chorus praising God.

4.

GOD'S "CALLED OUT" PEOPLE

Live such good lives among the pagans that, though they accuse you of doing wrong, they may see your good deeds and glorify God on the day he visits us.

—1 Peter 2:12

OVERVIEW

Those of us who are not called to do apostolic work still have a responsibility to reach others within our same culture. Our job is to live such good lives among nonbelievers that they'll be compelled to ask what makes us different.

To accomplish this task we must learn how much of evangelism is about how we live. As the old saying goes, "Actions speak louder than words." And the key to having our actions stand out is that they have to be done where others can see them. If all of our friends are followers of Christ, how will we make Christ known to those who don't believe?

In this lesson, you'll learn what lifestyle evangelism looks like, examine what it means to live "among the natives," and study the New Testament instructions for living such a life. Your goal is to evaluate your way of life and discover how you can interact with those outside God's kingdom.

So, what's the big deal?
Evangelism is as much about how we live as what we say. But many of us live in an insulated, subcultural pocket. All our friends share our faith, and we don't really know anyone who doesn't. The unbelievers we do rub shoulders with at work or school are little more than acquaintances. How can we minister to them with our lives if we never get close enough for them to know us?

1. Dictionary definitions of evangelism include such statements as "zealous preaching and dissemination of the gospel," and "missionary work or militant zeal for a cause." How would you define evangelism?

Jesus described one aspect of evangelism in the Great Commission—to "go and make disciples of all nations" (Matthew 28:19). But Peter described another kind, one of actions rather than words in the following passage.

> Live an exemplary life among the natives so that your actions will refute their prejudices. Then they'll be won over to God's side and be there to join in the celebration when he arrives. (1 Peter 2:12, MSG)

2. According to Peter, how else can we reach others for Christ?

Peter then went on to describe what "exemplary lives" should look like. The first area he addressed was civic life. His call to "submit to civil authorities" was made in the context of the Roman empire under Nero, a notorious and cruel tyrant. Peter's readers lived in dangerous circumstances. In their authoritarian society, they were accused of undermining the state by refusing to offer incense to the emperor. By refusing to comply with the law, they were in danger of being arrested and possibly executed.

Peter was not telling his readers—then or now—to compromise God's law or their consciences, but to obey the civil authorities in the everyday activities of their lives. Peter's readers were persecuted for their faith, and he stressed that persecution should be for obeying God rather than breaking civil laws or defying civil authority. Following Jesus is not an excuse to defy all authorities except God.

> Submit yourselves for the Lord's sake to every authority instituted among men: whether to the king, as the supreme authority, or to governors, who are sent by him to punish those who do wrong and to commend those who do right. For it is God's will that by doing good you should silence the ignorant talk of foolish men. Live as free men, but do not use your freedom as a cover-up for evil; live as servants of God. Show proper respect to everyone: Love the brotherhood of believers, fear God, honor the king.
> (1 Peter 2:13-17)

3. What kinds of authorities do you think fit Peter's description of "every authority instituted among men"?

4. a. In what ways is living a good life in the civic arena the same for us today as it was in Peter's day?

   b. How is it different?

5. What does it mean to live a good life in a democratic society where we can vote and have our freedom protected by law?

6. What kinds of behavior within a civic arena would draw unbelievers to Christ?

7. What kinds of public behavior among believers do you think drives people away from Christ?

Peter then addressed the relationships between slaves and masters. Many believers during Peter's time were household slaves. Obedience to kind masters was well and good, but Peter also encouraged respect for masters who were cruel and unjust.

While slavery is illegal in most countries today, many people use this passage as a guide for relationships between employers and employees. By showing respect and cooperation with our employers—whether kind or harsh—we can set a good example for coworkers and our boss.

> Slaves, submit yourselves to your masters with all respect, not only to those who are good and considerate, but also to those who are harsh. For it is commendable if a man bears up under the pain of unjust suffering because he is conscious of God. But how is it to your credit if you receive a beating for doing wrong and endure it? But if you suffer for doing good and you endure it, this is commendable before God. To this you were called, because Christ suffered for you, leaving you an example, that you should follow in his steps.
>
> "He committed no sin,
>   and no deceit was found in his mouth."

When they hurled their insults at him, he did not retaliate; when he suffered, he made no threats. Instead, he entrusted himself to him who judges justly. He himself bore our sins in his body on the tree, so that we might die to sins and live for righteousness; by his wounds you have been healed. For you were like sheep going astray, but now you have returned to the Shepherd and Overseer of your souls. (1 Peter 2:18-25)

8. How might a slave attract an unbelieving master to Christ?

9. How is that similar to or different from employer/employee relationships today?

10. What kinds of behavior in your workplace would draw a boss or coworker to Christ?

The next area Peter addressed was the relationship between husbands and wives. At the time of Peter's writing, when a man decided to follow Christ, he usually brought his entire family with him to the local gathering of believers. But when a woman became a believer, she often had to attend meetings alone. Under the laws of the day, a husband had complete authority over each member of the household and could prevent his wife from practicing her faith.

The instructions Peter gave were for those women whose freedom to practice their faith was in jeopardy. By being exemplary wives, they had the opportunity to win their husbands to Christ. Submission to their husbands was therefore not a state of servitude, but of cooperation out of love and respect for Christ.

> Wives, in the same way be submissive to your husbands so that, if any of them do not believe the word, they may be won over without words by the behavior of their wives, when they see the purity and reverence of your lives. Your beauty should not come from outward adornment, such as braided hair and the wearing of gold jewelry and fine clothes. Instead, it should be that of your inner self, the unfading beauty of a gentle and quiet spirit, which is of great worth in God's sight. For this is the way the holy women of the past who put their hope in God used to make themselves beautiful. They were submissive to their own husbands, like Sarah, who obeyed Abraham and called him her master. You are her daughters if you do what is right and do not give way to fear.
>
> Husbands, in the same way be considerate as you live with your wives, and treat them with respect as the weaker partner and as heirs with you of the gracious gift of life, so that nothing will hinder your prayers. (1 Peter 3:1-7)

11. a. How would Peter's advice to wives draw an unbelieving husband to Christ?

b. How would this kind of behavior affect those outside the family?

12. Similarly, how would Peter's advice to husbands affect those who saw it from outside the family?

13. What kinds of behaviors among family members today could be an effective witness to unbelievers?

For Further Study

The New Testament is full of additional instruction for how we are to live among those who don't believe. What do each of the following passages add to Peter's instruction for living a "good life"?

- ► 1 Corinthians 5:9-13
- ► Ephesians 6:5-9
- ► Philippians 1:27-30
- ► Philippians 2:14-16
- ► Colossians 4:5-6
- ► 1 Timothy 2:1-4
- ► 1 Timothy 3:1-7

 GROUP DISCOVERY   **(50-90 minutes)**

Let's Warm Up (10 minutes)

14. What does it usually take to change your opinion about something?
- ☐ Personal experience
- ☐ A close and trusted friend's opinion
- ☐ A new way of seeing something
- ☐ Facts
- ☐ A compelling testimony
- ☐ I seldom change my opinions
- ☐ Other (please explain):

Let's Talk (30-50 minutes)

15. Review your answers to the "On Your Own" section. What did you learn about evangelism? About living a "good life"?

Peter ended his instructions on living a good life "among the natives" by addressing how to relate to others we come into contact with. Peter knew firsthand that these were hard lessons to learn. Compassion and humility did not come naturally to him. Peter's natural tendency had been to say the first thing that came to mind (Mark 8:31-33, John 13:6-9). But as the Holy Spirit changed Peter's heart, he learned the value of treating others with dignity and respect. Read 1 Peter 3:8-16 aloud before moving on to the following questions.

16. How do you typically respond when insulted or attacked?

17. How does Peter say you should respond when others are unkind?

18. How would such a response affect nonbelievers who saw it?

19. What are some of the risks or costs to living as Peter describes?

20. a. What do you think Peter means when he says to "always be prepared to give an answer to everyone who asks you to give the reason for the hope you have"?

b. What is your answer?

21. a. Why do you suppose Peter didn't say his readers should aggressively witness to their families, coworkers, or friends?

b. How is aggressive witnessing different from having an answer prepared to give when you're asked about your faith?

22. The key to lifestyle evangelism is what Peter calls living "among the natives" (1 Peter 2:12, MSG). Unless we live among unbelievers and interact with them, they won't be able to see how our lives are different. As believers, we are not to be "of the world," but we are to be "in the world." Do you think it's possible to build meaningful relationships with unbelievers while following this teaching? Explain your answer.

23. In order to build relationships with unbelievers, you have to know some. It's tempting to build all of our friendships with others who also follow Christ. Where and how could you spend more time with unbelievers?

24. What hinders you from building relationships with unbelievers?
   ☐ Fear
   ☐ Not a priority
   ☐ Time
   ☐ Nothing in common
   ☐ My lifestyle never puts me in touch with them
   ☐ Other (please explain):

Let's Act (15-30 minutes)
25. Think about the parts of your life in which you interact with unbelievers. If there aren't many, how can you change your lifestyle to include regular contact with them?

26. What areas of your life can you share that will let them see Christ through your actions?

GROUP WORSHIP   **(15-30 minutes)**

27. Design your own worship time, focusing on the lessons learned through this chapter.

Let's Listen to God (15 minutes)

Throughout this study guide the question, "What do you think the Holy Spirit is saying to your group about . . . ?" is raised. Perhaps it seems presumptuous to claim to know what the Spirit is saying. Perhaps you are confident that you know, or maybe you are willing to settle for what you think the Spirit *ought* to be saying to your group.

Listening to the Spirit's voice is a skill your group can develop over time. It requires discipline and the willingness to cultivate certain attitudes and take certain risks. As you begin your time of listening to God, read aloud the following commitments. These are not once-for-all-time commitments; each one will require a process of commitment and recommitment by each group member.

▶ We acknowledge our own agendas, plans, philosophies, ideas, and paradigms, and we determine not to let them interfere with our relationship with God or with each other. We may not get this right all the time, but will keep it in mind every week as we meet.

▶ We commit ourselves to being open, honest, vulnerable, available, and transparent. Of course, if we're going to do this for real, we will have to deal with the relationship tensions and conflicts that arise. The result will be the beginning of authentic relationships.

▶ We present ourselves to God in humility, poverty of spirit, brokenness, contrition, and submission. God says He is near to these kinds of persons (Isaiah 57:15, 66:2). The prophet Azariah told the king and people of Judah:

> "The LORD is with you when you are with him. If you seek him, he will be found by you, but if you forsake him, he will forsake you. For a long time Israel was without the true God. . . . But in their distress they turned to the LORD, the God of Israel, and sought him, and he was found by them." (2 Chronicles 15:2-4)

Your agenda for this time of listening to God is to try to hear what God is saying through each group member as you share your thoughts on the following questions. Your challenge is to listen to God while talking to each other. Take a moment for silent prayer, then spend about fifteen minutes on the following:

28. After reading aloud the preceding three commitments, discuss what you sense the Holy Spirit communicating to your group about the following areas.

    ☐ Your worship and relationship with God

    ☐ Your relationships with each other

    ☐ Your relationships with those outside this group

29. Take a moment to close this conversation in prayer.

5.
THE MESSAGE ABOUT JESUS

Therefore let all Israel be assured of this: God has made this Jesus, whom you crucified, both Lord and Christ.
—Acts 2:36

OVERVIEW

Much of what we call the gospel today is a story about the life and work of Jesus. But the gospel is much more. It's an initiation into a way of life. Instead of sharing the gospel as a way of life, we often reduce it to an event, or being saved.

In the next two chapters we will look at how we can be prepared to give an answer for the hope we have. In this chapter we look at the essential elements of the gospel and how we often reduce the gospel to be a mere legal transaction saving us from hell. Then in the next chapter, we will examine how we often add to the gospel. In both chapters, your goal is to gain a clearer understanding of the gospel message.

So, what's the big deal?
As believers, we're called to share the gospel with others. But if we don't adequately understand the gospel, we can't adequately share it with others. So what exactly is the gospel?

ON YOUR OWN   (30-60 minutes)

1. How would you define the gospel?

The book of Acts records how the story of Jesus spread. After the Holy Spirit came at Pentecost, many people in the crowd were amazed and skeptical at the sight of the believers suddenly speaking in so many different languages. At their ridicule, Peter stood up and addressed the crowd, assuring them that these men were not drunk as the crowd supposed. He explained how Pentecost fulfilled Joel's prophesy of the Holy Spirit. Then Peter shared the gospel with the crowd. When his listeners heard the term "the Christ," they knew immediately that this was the king whom God had promised to send Israel, a king descended from David, Israel's greatest king. Every Jew had a picture in his mind of what the Christ was going to be like: a great warrior who would drive out the Roman oppressors and restore Israel to its days of glory. Dying was not part of anybody's picture of the Christ.

2. Read Acts 2:22-36, making a list as you go of words or phrases that define the gospel.

3. List the elements of the gospel that Peter presented to the crowd.

4. Why is each element important?

Jesus began His ministry in Galilee by preaching in synagogues. On one occasion He preached in the synagogue of His hometown, Nazareth.

> Jesus returned to Galilee in the power of the Spirit, and news about him spread through the whole countryside. He taught in their synagogues, and everyone praised him.
> He went to Nazareth, where he had been brought up, and on the Sabbath day he went into the synagogue, as was his custom. And he stood up to read.

The scroll of the prophet Isaiah was handed to him. Unrolling it, he found the place where it is written:

> "The Spirit of the Lord is on me,
>> because he has anointed me
>> to preach good news to the poor.
> He has sent me to proclaim freedom for the prisoners
>> and recovery of sight for the blind,
> to release the oppressed,
>> to proclaim the year of the Lord's favor."

Then he rolled up the scroll, gave it back to the attendant and sat down. The eyes of everyone in the synagogue were fastened on him, and he began by saying to them, "Today this scripture is fulfilled in your hearing." (Luke 4:14-21)

5. Gospel is an old English word meaning "good news." This passage is one of Jesus' earliest statements of the good news or gospel. Compare it to Peter's account of the gospel in Acts 2. How are the two versions similar? How do they differ?

☐ Similarities

☐ Differences

6. What do you think Jesus' readers thought He meant by "freedom for the prisoners" and "release the oppressed"?

7. What do you think Jesus meant?

In Romans 8, Paul describes the good news of Jesus as it relates to all of creation. The liberation he talks about is not just freeing people from political oppression, psychological oppression, or other kinds of bondage, but liberation for the whole universe.

> Now if we are children, then we are heirs—heirs of God and co-heirs with Christ, if indeed we share in his sufferings in order that we may also share in his glory.
>
> I consider that our present sufferings are not worth comparing with the glory that will be revealed in us. The creation waits in eager expectation for the sons of God to be revealed. For the creation was subjected to frustration, not by its own choice, but by the will of the one who subjected it, in hope that the creation itself will be liberated from its bondage to decay and brought into the glorious freedom of the children of God.
>
> We know that the whole creation has been groaning as in the pains of childbirth right up to the present time. Not only so, but we ourselves, who have the firstfruits of the Spirit, groan inwardly as we wait eagerly for our adoption as sons, the redemption of our bodies. For in this hope we were saved. But hope that is seen is no hope at all. Who hopes for what he already has? But if we hope for what we do not yet have, we wait for it patiently.
>
> In the same way, the Spirit helps us in our weakness. We do not know what we ought to pray for, but the Spirit himself intercedes for us with groans that words cannot express. And he who searches our hearts knows the mind of the Spirit, because the Spirit intercedes for the saints in accordance with God's will. (Romans 8:17-27)

8. What good news does Jesus have for the cosmos?

9. What does this have to do with the gospel as we might explain it to people?

10. From reading these accounts of the gospel, how would you now define the gospel?

For Further Study
The Gospels (Matthew, Mark, Luke, and John) are eyewitness accounts of Jesus' life and ministry on earth. Since the gospel is the story of Jesus, it's important to know the details about Jesus' life. Pick one of the Gospels to read during the next week. If you read three or four chapters a day, you should easily be able to finish in a week. Mark is the shortest Gospel; Luke is the longest. Keep a journal of what you learn about Jesus from your reading.

 GROUP DISCOVERY (50-90 minutes)

Let's Warm Up (10 minutes)
11. Other than the gospel, what's the best news you've ever received? How did it change your life?

Let's Talk (30-50 minutes)

12. Discuss your answers to the "On Your Own" questions. What did you learn about the gospel? Did your definition of the gospel change from your study? If so, how?

Many people see salvation as strictly a legal transaction. Once you're saved, that's it. You're assured eternity in heaven and can stop worrying about eternal condemnation. But salvation is only the beginning of the gospel. As Peter ended his message to the crowd on Pentecost, he told them what to do if they believed what he had said. At first glance it seems pretty simple.

> Repent and be baptized, every one of you, in the name of Jesus Christ for the forgiveness of your sins. And you will receive the gift of the Holy Spirit. (Acts 2:38)

13. What does Peter say we must do to be forgiven?

Repentance is defined as real and lasting change of mind and heart. Some of the confusion surrounding repentance can be traced to translation difficulties. Latin versions of the Bible translated the Greek word *metanoia* (a change of mind or purpose) "to exercise penitence." This way of translating suggests paying for your sin, but not changing your thoughts or actions.

14. How is that similar to or different from the picture most people have in their heads about repentance?

15. Do you think repentance is a one-time act or an on-going process? Explain your answer.

16. What is the purpose of God's gift of the Holy Spirit? (The following passages may help you answer this question.)

> But the Counselor, the Holy Spirit, whom the Father will send in my name, will teach you all things and will remind you of everything I have said to you. (John 14:26)

> I pray that out of his glorious riches he may strengthen you with power through his Spirit in your inner being, so that Christ may dwell in your hearts through faith. And I pray that you, being rooted and established in love, may have power, together with all the saints, to grasp how wide and long and high and deep is the love of Christ. (Ephesians 3:16-18)

17. Why is the Holy Spirit an important part of the gospel?

18. What obstacles exist when sharing the gospel with unbelievers?

Let's Act (15-30 minutes)
Imagine that you've been asked to give an account for the hope you have.

> While at work one day, Bob approaches you and says he's noticed that you're different. Bob has had little interaction with other believers, has never been to church, and hasn't

read the Bible. He can't put his finger on it, but there's definitely something about you he can't figure out. "What is it?" he asks.

"Well, Bob," you answer, "it's Jesus. The Holy Spirit convicted me of my sin and my separation from God. But because Jesus died on the cross and rose again, He paid the price for my sin and restored me to a right relationship with God. I asked Jesus to come into my heart and He gave me the gift of His Holy Spirit. With the Holy Spirit's help, I try to live like Jesus and allow Him to reign in my life."

19. Do you think Bob understood your answer? If not, why not?

20. How could you change your answer to an account of the gospel that Bob would understand and relate to? "Well, Bob. . . ."

 GROUP WORSHIP   **(15-30 minutes)**

21. Begin by reading 1 Corinthians 15:1-11 together.

22. If your group is so inclined, sing an appropriate hymn or chorus.

23. Thank God together for the good news about Jesus. Praise Him for His mercy and His love. Pray that you would clearly understand the gospel and be able to effectively share it with those who ask. Think back to last week and the unbeliever you've been praying for. Pray that God would give you an opportunity to share the gospel with that person.

6.

THE ADVANCEMENT OF THE MESSAGE

*Now then, why do you try to test God by putting on the
necks of the disciples a yoke that neither we nor our
fathers have been able to bear? No! We believe it is
through the grace of our Lord Jesus that we are saved,
just as they are.*

—Acts 15:10-11

OVERVIEW

Just as we have a tendency to reduce the gospel, we
also have a tendency to add to it. Instead of talking about the good
news of Jesus, we sometimes focus on extras—where you go to church,
how you vote, what you wear, the kinds of movies you see, and so on.

In this chapter, we'll look at those things we add to the gospel that
hinder its effectiveness in reaching others. Your goal is to gain a clearer
understanding of what the gospel is and what it doesn't include.

So, what's the big deal?
When we add to the gospel, we often scare unbelievers away.
Suddenly, the good news about Jesus becomes a massive system of do's
and don'ts. To reach people with the gospel, we need to present the
gospel—no more and no less. But it's difficult to see the things that we
add to the gospel because they're often central to how we ourselves
worship and live.

1. How comfortable are you with sharing the gospel?
☐ Very comfortable. I do it so often it feels very natural.
☐ The thought makes me slightly nervous, but if I prepare in advance I know I'll be fine.
☐ I'm comfortable with the idea, but the opportunity doesn't come my way very often.
☐ Uneasy. The mere thought makes me break out in a sweat!
☐ It's not something I've thought about. I've never really done it and guess I'll find out when the time comes.
☐ Other (please explain):

How did the gospel spread? Beginning with a small band of simple, provincial disciples, the gospel was planted and still growing throughout the whole Roman world fifty years later. How did the early church keep the gospel pure?

By the time of Jesus centuries of tradition had shaped Jewish practice. However, God's self-revelation in Jesus and the Holy Spirit shook the assumptions upon which Jewish customs were founded. The Jewish believers in and around Jerusalem transitioned gradually to a Christ-centered message. They maintained many aspects of their tradition while reinterpreting the meanings according to their fulfillment in Christ.

By contrast, Jewish believers outside Palestine were less steeped in Jewish tradition and more accustomed to Greek ways, while Gentile believers had no interest at all in maintaining Jewish customs. They found Jewish dietary laws annoying, and they considered circumcision barbaric—bodily mutilation was unthinkable to the Greeks. Hence, they rejected many Jewish rituals and made a clear distinction between what was culturally Jewish and what was central to following Christ. These distinctions caused conflict with the traditionalists.

To the Jewish believers, their cultural lifestyle was simply part of following the Messiah. But the Gentiles wanted to follow Jesus without adopting Jewish culture. Things came to a head when some Jews from

Palestine traveled to Paul's home base in Syrian Antioch to insist that the Gentile believers there conform to Jewish customs. Paul and Barnabas, leaders of the missionary efforts to the Gentiles, challenged that teaching.

The two sides agreed to take the question to the leaders of the original community in Jerusalem. The council in Jerusalem was faced with the same question we are considering—what is central to the gospel message?

2. Read Acts 15:1-35. What had the traditionalists added to the gospel?

3. Why do you think the traditionalists add things to the gospel?

4. Why did Peter argue against adding to the gospel (verses 7-11)?

5. James, the brother of Jesus, was well-known for his strict adherence to Jewish law. What was his opinion about the issue at hand (verses 13-21)?

6. What are some of the items we add to the gospel today?

7. Why do you think we add these kinds of things to the gospel?

8. How do you think it affects the gospel when we add things to it?

9. The council in Jerusalem sent a letter (Acts 15:22-30) responding to the Gentile believers' questions about Jewish customs being forced on them. What were the customs the council said the Gentile believers needed to adopt?

10. The council settled on these four issues because they caused the most tension between Jewish and Gentile believers. The Jews found these Gentile customs so offensive that their disagreement dominated any meeting of the two groups. Are these restrictions still applicable today? Why or why not?

11. Change isn't always immediate—especially when it involves attitudes and behaviors. All too often we expect people to change and be acceptable before following Jesus. But God accepts us as we are—fallen, sinful people. It's His desire to then mold us into the image of Christ—something we can never do on our own. How would you explain this kind of change to an unbeliever?

12. List any questions you have about the situation in Acts 15.

For Further Study
Read through the book of Galatians this week, jotting down the different elements those believers were adding to the gospel. Reflect on what might have influenced them to add each one, then consider what contemporary parallels might be drawn. If Paul were writing an epistle to the members of your group (or church), what additions to the gospel would he identify? Share your thoughts with the group.

 GROUP DISCOVERY   **(50-90 minutes)**

Let's Warm Up (10 minutes)
13. What's the strangest thing anyone has ever asked you about your faith in Christ?

14. Discuss your answers to the "On Your Own" questions. What did you learn about the gospel? What questions could the group help answer from the Acts passage?

The story of Naaman in the Old Testament is a good example of presenting the gospel without an impossible list of do's and don'ts.

In Naaman's time, leprosy was one of the most feared diseases—much like AIDS today. Some forms of the disease were very contagious, incurable, and could lead to death. Since Naaman still held his position in the army, chances are his leprosy was in its early stages. Eventually, however, Naaman faced expulsion from his position and his family, as lepers were often sent outside the city to die.

When Naaman realized that Elisha was his only chance for a cure, he immediately left for Israel. Accustomed to being treated with respect, Naaman was dismayed that Elisha didn't even bother to come out of his house. Imagine his reaction to being told to go wash in a dirty river. But when Naaman finally humbled himself and was cured, he was convinced that the God of Israel was the only true God.

One of Naaman's jobs was to help his king bow before the idols in the temple of Rimmon. He questioned Elisha about this and asked for God's forgiveness for this job he was required to carry out. Read 2 Kings 5:1-19, and note Elisha's response.

15. Why did Naaman want God's permission to bow to Rimmon?

16. What was Elisha's response?

17. Why is Elisha's response so significant?

18. Does his response surprise you? Why, or why not?

19. Why do you suppose Elisha didn't tell Naaman not to bow to Rimmon?

20. What similar kinds of things are people concerned about today when they hear the gospel?

Imagine that Mark, your next-door neighbor, notices a difference when comparing your lifestyle to his. Interested in hearing more about your faith, Mark asks what it means to follow Christ.

> "Well, Mark," you reply, "first of all, your life has got to change. You really need to fellowship with other believers on Sundays and get involved in a Bible study. You're going to have to quit your bartending job and either marry your girlfriend or make her move out. You ought to vote Republican since they're pro-life, and you should reevaluate your tastes in entertainment—R-rated movies are definitely out, and most of the programs on television contain such heavy sexual innuendo or violence that you're better off not watching at all. Oh, and you have to give 10 percent of your income to the church. There's more, but we can get into that later."

21. Describe what you envision Mark's response looking like.

22. How would you approach Mark's lifestyle issues? What things need to change immediately and what things will you trust God to gradually change about him?

23. Do you think Jesus would tell Mark to "go in peace" as Elisha told Naaman? Why, or why not?

24. After this session, would you change or add to your definition of the gospel? If so, how?

Let's Act (15 minutes)
25. As a group, examine your understanding of the gospel. What cultural traditions or assumptions have you added to the "good news?"

26. What kind of support would you like from this group as you look ahead to sharing the gospel with others?

GROUP WORSHIP   (15-30 minutes)

27. Design your own worship experience from the material in this lesson.

Let's Listen to God (15 minutes)

28. After reading aloud the three commitments on pages 53, discuss what you sense the Holy Spirit is communicating to your group about the following areas.

☐ Your worship and relationship with God

☐ Your relationships with each other

☐ Your relationships with those outside this group

29. Take a moment to close this conversation in prayer.

7.

DOING JUSTICE AND ACTING RIGHTEOUSLY

And what does the LORD require of you? To act justly and
to love mercy and to walk humbly with your God.

—Micah 6:8

OVERVIEW

Righteousness and justice (*tsedeqah u mishpat* in Hebrew) is a figure of speech in which two Hebrew words connected by a conjunction form a single complex idea. The concepts behind these two words run throughout the Old Testament. When we come to the New Testament, a single Greek word is used to capture both ideas. For example, Jesus taught us "to seek first his kingdom and his righteousness (justice)" (Matthew 6:33).

In this session we're going to explore the distributive side of righteousness and justice, or "social justice," rather than retributive or legal justice. Social justice is simply living and acting as God Himself would. God is just and righteous, and justice and righteousness are the foundations of His throne (Psalm 89:14). By looking at biblical examples of justice, we can understand how we as believers can practice justice—another form of living out the gospel—in our surroundings.

So, what's the big deal?

Many believers are so focused on evangelism that they tend to ignore justice as an integral part of the gospel. The fact that God cares about justice and sent Jesus to do justice and live righteously is very much a part of the good news.

1. What comes to mind when you think of justice?

2. Is justice something you think about often? Explain.

3. Why do you think injustice occurs? (What are some of the reasons or motives behind it?)

The prophet Isaiah was not popular. His message to the Israelites was often brutally honest and scathing. But as his ministry reached its end, Isaiah's message was laced with promise. If Israel obeyed God, He would bring blessing.

In the passage below, Isaiah describes the kind of justice God expects. Isaiah addresses the Jews' custom of fasting from food and drink as a way of demonstrating their devotion to God. That's fine, says God, but there's a more important way of demonstrating devotion. Read Isaiah 58:6-14 before moving on to the following questions.

4. According to Isaiah, what actions does justice require?

5. Do you think these actions are still applicable today? Explain.

6. What are some areas of justice that you've practiced in the past?
   □ Shared food, shelter, and clothing with those in need
   □ Volunteered in a social service agency
   □ Served as a board member for a local nonprofit
   □ Reached out to family members when they've needed help
   □ Run for political office
   □ Refrained from malicious talk or accusing others of wrong
   □ Given up a salary increase so lower paid employees could
     receive a just wage
   □ Other (please explain):

7. What is promised for those who act justly?

8. Why is God so concerned with justice?

9. The hungry, the poor, and the oppressed are mentioned more than once in this passage. Why do you think God has a special concern for these people?

10. What are some of the ways you can obey Isaiah's teaching?

11. Of the ideas you listed, which are most appealing to you?

Read the following passage from Ezekiel about Sodom. Genesis 19 tells how God destroyed Sodom because of the wickedness of its inhabitants.

> "Now this was the sin of your sister Sodom: She and her daughters were arrogant, overfed and unconcerned; they did not help the poor and needy. . . . Therefore I did away with them as you have seen." (Ezekiel 16:49-50)

12. What's your reaction to these verses? For example, are you surprised at the reason why God destroyed Sodom?

13. Does this passage affect your thinking about how you approach justice? If so, how?

For Further Study
The Old Testament is full of God's views on justice and righteousness. Pick several of these passages to study. What do you learn about God's justice from them?

- ► Exodus 23:2
- ► Exodus 23:6
- ► Deuteronomy 16:18-20
- ► Deuteronomy 24:17
- ► Psalm 33:4-5
- ► Psalm 82:3-4
- ► Psalm 103:6
- ► Psalm 106:3

- ► Proverbs 21:3
- ► Proverbs 28:5
- ► Proverbs 29:7
- ► Isaiah 1:17
- ► Isaiah 28:16-17
- ► Isaiah 56:1
- ► Jeremiah 9:23-24

 GROUP DISCOVERY (50-90 minutes)

Let's Warm Up (10 minutes)
14. When asked for money by someone on the street, how do you usually respond?

Let's Talk (30-50 minutes)
15. Review your answers to the "On Your Own" questions. What did you learn about justice? About God?

We've established that justice is important to God and something that He requires of His followers. But how does justice actually happen?

Dr. Edward Kuhlmann, professor of social work at Eastern College, suggests four complementary approaches to doing justice: individual evangelism, caring community, social service, and social reform.[1]

Evangelism

Injustice in society is the result of individual sins such as greed, lying, cheating, and discrimination. Widespread problems are the result of multitudes of people committing that sin.

Because injustice can be traced back to individual sins, one solution to injustice is to change people one person at a time. This change is best accomplished by communicating the gospel to individuals. Through discipling and the work of the Holy Spirit, they will learn to change their sinful behavior. The cumulative effect of these behavior changes will gradually transform society and eliminate injustice.

16. Do you agree with the thinking behind evangelism as one solution to injustice? Why, or why not?

17. Do you see evidence that this approach changes the injustice found in society?

Caring Community

Another approach to change in society occurs through caring communities. As people join the Body of Christ through organizational forms like local churches, communities, cell groups, and extended families, they are nurtured into spiritual health and their problems are addressed.

The rationale for this approach is that, under the direction of the Holy Spirit, the love and concern of a caring community over-flows to both believers and unbelievers. Over time, society is transformed through these groups and injustice is eliminated.

18. Do you see evidence that caring communities change society and solve injustice? If so, describe it.

19. Do you agree with the thinking behind this approach to solving injustice? Why, or why not?

Social Service

A third approach to doing justice in society is to organize programs of social service. By directly delivering services that meet tangible needs, the poor, widows, fatherless, victims, foreigners, and all other oppressed peoples are helped. These services aren't just pro-vided by governmental agencies, but are often done through private organizations like crisis-pregnancy centers, children's agen-cies, prisoner assistance programs, churches, et cetera.

This approach is an organized application of the neighborli-ness described in the parable of the Good Samaritan (Luke 10:25-37). It does not negate the necessity of individual initiative or the support of caring communities, but it does stress organized programs or efforts for bringing justice to address the needs of the oppressed.

20. a. What kinds of social services operate where you live?

b. Do you think that social services are part of the answer to injustice? Why, or why not?

21. As a believer, what is your responsibility to support or create social service agencies in your area?

Social Reform

A fourth approach to doing justice suggests that processes such as industrialization and urbanization have produced a society that is marked by incredible complexity. One outcome of this complexity is that laws, policies, and programs can propagate injustice.

As a result, injustice continues until the societal structures are changed through legal or political means. As followers of Christ seek to abolish injustice, they should be actively involved in social reform. (For example, slavery was abolished in the United States through the social reform of those concerned about the inequality and poor treatment suffered by African Americans.)

22. a. What are some examples you've seen or read about social reform?

b. What were the results?

23. Do you agree that believers should be active in seeking social reform? Why, or why not?

24. These approaches to injustice are not meant to be exclusive, but simultaneous. Which ones do you lean toward?

25. What about them do you find true or appealing?

26. How does reaching out to others by promoting justice embody the gospel?

Let's Act (15-30 minutes)

27. Go back to question 10 in the "On Your Own" section. As a group, identify areas of injustice you feel a strong desire to address.

28. a. How can you become involved?

    b. Which type of approach to injustice does that involvement fall under?

29. List some of the things that might get in the way of fulfilling your good intentions to practice justice?

30. Begin by reading Micah 6:8 together and meditating on God's plan for your lives.

> He has showed you, O man, what is good. And what does the Lord require of you? To act justly and to love mercy and to walk humbly with your God. (Micah 6:8)

31. Design the rest of your worship time. Ask God to show you ways you can show justice to those around you.

Let's Listen to God (15 minutes)

32. After reading aloud the three commitments on pages 53, discuss what you sense the Holy Spirit is communicating to your group about the following areas.

☐ Your worship and relationship with God

☐ Your relationships with each other

☐ Your relationships with those outside this group

33. Take a moment to close this conversation in prayer.

---

1. Dr. Edward Kuhlmann, "A Taxonomy of Christian Social Mission," *The paraclete* (Journal of the National Association of Christians in Social Work), Winter 1976, Vol. 3, No. 2, pp. 53-68.

8.
LET'S PERSONALIZE OUTREACH

In this session and the next, you will review and apply the lessons you have learned in sessions 2–7. In this session you will focus on personal lessons and applications, while session 9 will focus on group applications. As you prepare for your group meeting, remember to pray frequently. Some inventory work will help you select the one key truth from sessions 2–7 that is most urgent for you personally. Then your group will help you think through appropriate action steps and life changes you can pursue. Your goal will be to settle on one key truth and the action you can take to build it into your life.

So what's the big deal?
It's better to be obedient in just one area about which God is convicting you than to fill up a workbook full of good intentions about several truths, none of which you obey or profit from.

ON YOUR OWN (30-60 minutes)

1. What changes are you beginning to see in your relationship with God as a result of this study?

☐ Any mistakes you are avoiding?

☐ Any attitudes you are changing?

☐ Any areas of new freedom in Christ?

☐ Any changes in the way you view God?

☐ Any new ways you feel or things you do when you spend time with God?

2. Review what you have studied and discussed in sessions 2 through 7. Try to state one or two truths that stand out to you as most important in each session. For example, you might write for session 7, "Both justice and evangelism are essential aspects of living the gospel."

☐ Session 2

☐ Session 3

☐ Session 4

☐ Session 5

☐ Session 6

☐ Session 7

3. You may have repeated yourself in question 2, circling around the
   same one or two truths that jump out at you from every session. If
   so, it may be that the Holy Spirit has put His finger on an area of
   focus. Take a moment to pray about your list of truths. Put a star
   beside the one that you think is most important for you to address
   in the near future. Or, combine several of the truths into one, and
   state it below. (Don't get sidetracked trying to summarize all of
   your truths into one overarching thesis. The point is to pick one
   limited idea that you can reasonably grasp and focus on.)

4. How has this truth affected your thinking and behavior so far?

5. How do you think the Holy Spirit would like this truth to affect your life—your thoughts, feelings, and actions?

Be prepared to share your key truth and its effects with your group. They will help you formulate a plan for integrating that truth into your life and acting on it. They will also help keep you accountable to the degree that you allow them to do so. You're not in this alone!

GROUP DISCOVERY (50-90 minutes)

Let's Warm Up (10 minutes)

6. What is one thing you have gained from this group during the past seven sessions? What is one thing for which you are grateful?

Let's Talk (45-80 minutes)

Plan your time so that you have at least five minutes for each person to share his or her truth and receive help in formulating a plan of action. Ten minutes each would be even better, but that might require going overtime. Be sure that no one is shortchanged of this opportunity for help.

7. Read to your group your key truth, how it has affected you so far, and how you think the Spirit would like it to affect you. Then, with help from the group, come up with a plan for integrating your key truth into your life. Ask yourselves the following questions as you help each other plan your strategies:

☐ Is the key truth clear?
☐ What results or outcomes would you like to see from this plan of action?
☐ Are the action steps specific and realistic?
☐ Not all action steps in the spiritual realm are quantifiable. For example, praying for thirty minutes a day is quantifiable, but genuinely opening your heart to God in prayer is not. How will you know if the changes you are pursuing are really happening?

Here is an example of a plan that is practical, specific, measurable, and clear:

My biggest problem regarding outreach is that I simply don't take the time to be involved with unbelievers in my world. I motor around in my self-contained social system, basically ignoring those who aren't part of it. This week I'm going to invite my coworker, John, to have lunch with me. During that lunch, I'm going to ask questions about his life. I'm wondering, "What does a guy like John need?" Taking initiative in relationships is hard for me, and asking personal questions is really hard. So someone from this group is going to check in with me on Friday to see whether I've gotten it together with John. I'm going to pray about this every morning at the beginning of my workday until I follow through on it. I'll report back to the group next week on what happened.

Write your plan here, continuing on the top of the next page:

8. List anything you have committed to do for someone else in your group:

9. Use this space to list the other group members' key truths (you will need these to do your personal preparation for session 9):

GROUP WORSHIP   **(15-30 minutes)**

10. Design and implement your own time of worship. Be sure to include prayer about your key truth and your plans for applying it.

9.
LET'S GROW TOGETHER THROUGH OUTREACH

OVERVIEW

The work you do this session will be similar to session 8 in that you will review and apply the lessons you have learned in sessions 2–7. In this session your goal is to come up with an application for your whole group, whereas last time the focus was on personal application.

Planning group applications requires hard work. You will be thinking in areas that may be different from anything you have tried before. Six areas have been selected to help you evaluate your group's progress.

So what's the big deal?
If you persevere, you will achieve powerful results. You will be growing not just as individuals but also as a community of believers.

ON YOUR OWN (30-60 minutes)

Throughout the course of these studies, you have had experiences that contributed to your sense of community. Take a few minutes to assess the progress and contributions your group has made in spiritual sensitivity, worship dynamics, relational intimacy, functional interdependence, mission focus, and sphere of influence. This assessment procedure will help you evaluate your group's progress and help you plan for your future relationships.

1. **Ability to listen to the Holy Spirit.** In a group with high sensitivity to the Spirit, you will observe unity and peace created by the Spirit, or you will observe people allowing the Spirit to disrupt their complacency and challenge their assumptions. On a scale of 1 (low) to 5 (high), how would you rate your group's sensitivity, receptivity, and responsiveness to the Holy Spirit's leadership?

1	2	3	4	5
low				high

2. **Worship dynamics.** God is the central focus in worship. Recall your worship times in the preceding sessions. In a group with "rich" worship dynamics you can expect to find a sense of God's majestic presence with you, variety, and everyone participating and contributing. On a scale of 1 (poor) to 5 (rich), how would you assess the overall quality of your group's worship experience?

1	2	3	4	5
poor				rich

3. **Relational intimacy.** The Bible is full of relational terms such as love, forgiveness, acceptance, reconciliation, and bearing one another's burdens. As you experience these conditions, your group will grow in relational intimacy. Evidences of "deep" intimacy are high levels of trust, vulnerability, transparency, honesty, and mutual commitment. On a scale of 1 (shallow) to 5 (deep), how would you assess your group's level of intimacy?

1	2	3	4	5
shallow				deep

4. **Functional interdependence.** The church is the body of Christ, a living organism with many members. Your small group functions like a system in that body, working interdependently with other systems and their members. Not only that, each member of your group is gifted to perform specific tasks that contribute to the overall internal functions of your group. On a scale of 1 (harsh, grating) to 5 (sweet, synchronized), how well are the members of

your community working together toward a common task, and how harmoniously is your community working alongside others?

1	2	3	4	5
harsh, grating				sweet, synchronized

5. **Mission focus.** Christian communities can easily become self-absorbed. This happens when they turn a deaf ear or a blind eye to what's on God's heart and, instead, focus their attention on themselves. The result is a diminished heart for the world that God loves and gave His Son to die for. God uses groups to reach into every nook and cranny of the world. On a scale of 1 (self-absorbed) to 5 (other-focused), how motivated is your group to looking beyond itself and fulfilling God's mission to reach the world?

1	2	3	4	5
self-absorbed				other-focused

6. **Sphere of influence.** God's mission is global in scope, including all kinds of people—rich and poor, men and women, young and old, Black, White, Hispanic, Asian, et cetera. Although we are to be open to new ministry opportunities, God often calls a community to minister within its specific sphere of influence. This sphere sets limits that sharpen your focus. On a scale of 1 (confused, non-existent) to 5 (sharply focused), how clear is it to your community who God has called you to minister to?

1	2	3	4	5
confused				focused

7. Review all the truths and life applications that you and your fellow group members identified last time. What is the one truth from these studies that you feel is most relevant for your whole group collectively? (This may be different from what is most significant to you personally.)

GROUP DISCOVERY ⟳ **(50-90 minutes)**

Let's Warm Up (10 minutes)

8. What is one way this group has helped you become equipped and motivated to reach out to unbelievers?

Let's Talk (30-45 minutes)

9. Share progress on personal applications from the last session. Are you helping each other follow through on your commitments? How so? Thank God for the progress He has already made among you.

10. Remember, community building is a process. Some members of your group may desire greater intimacy, and some may feel threatened by the intimacy already achieved. God is still at work in your group in the six areas you assessed on pages 90-91. He is molding you into a vehicle fit for Him to use however He wills. Review the six areas of assessment and compare answers as a group. Pay special attention to major differences in your evaluations. How do you account for these differences?

11. Discuss what each of you thinks is the one significant truth most relevant to your group (identified in question 7). Try to come to a group consensus of the one truth and its implications for your group. To reach that consensus, here are some helpful hints:
    - ☐ Begin with prayer, asking God to clarify your thinking.
    - ☐ List the truth from each individual on a chart or white board.
    - ☐ Look for duplications and related themes. Consolidate and combine where possible.

☐ Build consensus on one truth. Sometimes related thoughts can be combined to better reflect the overall truth but beware of stringing ideas together into a broad, complicated conglomeration.

☐ Don't worry about a perfect statement. Blend the ideas of each person in the group to arrive at the consensus position. (Designate someone in the group who has an aptitude with words to edit for clarity and length. Take the statement home to polish it up, if necessary.)

12. Write your group truth here.

13. Next you will plan how to integrate this truth into your group life, much as you did for each individual group member last time. Your first step will be prayer. Take five minutes to ask God to lead you in this process. You might ask, "Lord, how would you like our group to put this truth into practice?" or "God, what would you like our community to become?" Listen quietly. As you have thoughts or impressions, either make mental notes or jot them down.

14. Write three headings on newsprint or a white board: God, One Another, Others. Under the first heading, list ways in which this truth should affect your group's relationship with God. Under the second heading, list ways in which this truth should affect your relationships with each other, and so on.

God	One Another	Others

15. Now brainstorm a fourth list: things you can do to put this truth into practice in your group. Call out ideas without evaluating or criticizing any of them.

16. After five or ten minutes, stop and sort the ideas into short-range steps and long-range steps. Edit them so that each one is a realistic, doable action that lends itself to accountability. Who will do what, by when, where, and for/with whom? Weed out any impractical ideas. Try to come up with at least one short-range and one long-range step that meet these standards.
    ☐ What is it?
    ☐ Who will do what?
    ☐ By when?
    ☐ Where?
    ☐ For/with whom?

    a. Short-range steps

    b. Long-range steps

Because learning to implement this truth as a community is so important, you should commit yourselves to take as many sessions as needed to work out your group application. Place a higher priority on implementing your plan rather than moving on to another study.

17. Design and implement your own time of worship. Be sure to include prayer about your key truth and your plans for applying it. Also, thank God for what you have received from this study. Celebrate your time together, both your past and your future.

If you set out to identify the core elements of the Christian life, what would your list include?

After ten years of Bible study involving thousands of believers from countries all around the world, The Navigators' SCRIPTURAL ROOTS OF LIFE team saw a few basic themes emerge over and over again:

WORSHIP
Worship: Honoring God in All of Life
(ISBN: 1-57683-007-1; 9 sessions; 96 pages)

COMMUNITY
Relationships: Resolving Conflict and Building Community
(ISBN: 1-57683-023-3; 9 sessions; 96 pages)

INTIMACY WITH GOD
Intimacy: Pursuing Intimacy with God
(ISBN: 1-57683-010-1; 9 sessions; 96 pages)

BECOMING LIKE CHRIST
Christlikeness: Committing Ourselves to be Changed by God
(ISBN: 1-57683-006-3; 9 sessions; 96 pages)

THE TRINITY
Restoration: Discovering How God Meets Our Deepest Needs
(ISBN: 1-57683-009-8; 9 sessions; 96 pages)

THE UNSEEN WORLD
Warfare: Discovering the Reality of the Unseen World
(ISBN: 1-57683-026-8; 9 sessions; 96 pages)

SHARING THE FAITH
Outreach: Sharing the Real Gospel with the World
(ISBN: 1-57683-012-8; 9 sessions; 96 pages)

WORK
Work: Serving God on the Job
(ISBN: 1-57683-024-1; 9 sessions; 96 pages)

Designed to foster close-knit community within your group, the FOUNDATIONS FOR CHRISTIAN LIVING series is a great way to grow strong in faith, life, and love for God. Available at your local Christian bookstore. Or call 1-800-366-7788 to order.

NAVPRESS
BRINGING TRUTH TO LIFE